Botanical Artistry

Julia Trickey is an award-winning botanical artist and experienced tutor of some twenty years. She is particularly drawn to less-than-perfect specimens such as fading flowers, autumnal leaves and seed heads, often painting them larger than life. She has been awarded four RHS gold medals amongst many other awards. Julia has exhibited her watercolours all over the world, and her work is held in the RHS Lindley Library and The Shirley Sherwood Collection, London, the Hunt Institute for Botanical Documentation, Pittsburgh, PA, and the Chelsea Physic Garden Archives, London, as well as many private collections. She has written articles for national art magazines and resources and online tutorials for students of botanical art. She currently tutors botanical art classes in the beautiful historic city of Bath, UK, and leads workshops for botanical art groups around the country and beyond.

Botanical Art Porfolios

Botanical Art Portfolios is a new series featuring distinguished botanical artists, their work and their inspiration. Intentionally both beautiful and useful, these handy-sized paperbacks are designed to be taken anywhere, referred to, collected and gazed at. Each book will bring out the personality of its individual artist, showcase their work and share why they love what they do, explain their choice of subjects, the distinct techniques they have developed, and their failures as well as their successes. *Botanical Artistry* by Julia Trickey, the Series Editor, is the first to be published. Three more titles have been commissioned and others are in the pipeline.

See http://tworiverspress.com/botanical_art_portfolios for more information.

Also published by Two Rivers Press

The Greenwood Trees: History, folklore and uses of Britain's trees by Christina Hart-Davies

Reading Abbey and the Abbey Quarter by Peter Durrant and John Painter

Reading's Bayeux Tapestry by Reading Museum

A Coming of Age: Celebrating 18 Years of Botanical Painting by the Eden Project Florilegium Society by Ros Franklin

A Wild Plant Year: History, folklore and uses of Britain's flora by Christina Hart-Davies

Silchester: Life on the Dig by Jenny Halstead & Michael Fulford

Caught on Camera: Reading in the 70s by Terry Allsop

Plant Portraits by Post: Post & Go British Flora by Julia Trickey

Allen W. Seaby: Art and Nature by Martin Andrews & Robert Gillmor

Cover Birds by Robert Gillmor

An Artist's Year in the Harris Garden by Jenny Halstead

Caversham Court Gardens: A Heritage Guide by Friends of Caversham Court Gardens

Birds, Blocks & Stamps: Post & Go Birds of Britain by Robert Gillmor

Down by the River: The Thames and Kennet in Reading by Gillian Clark

Botanical Artistry

Plants, projects & processes

Julia Trickey

TWO RIVERS PRESS

First published in the UK in 2019 by Two Rivers Press
7 Denmark Road, Reading RG1 5PA
www.tworiverspress.com

ISBN 978-1-909747-45-6

2 3 4 5 6 7 8 9

Two Rivers Press is represented in the UK by Inpress Ltd and distributed by NBNi.

Cover design by Nadja Guggi with an illustration by Julia Trickey
Text design by Nadja Guggi and typeset in Parisine

Printed and bound in Great Britain by Gomer Press, Ceredigion

Acknowledgements

I feel privileged to be working with Two Rivers Press on this, the first in a series of books showcasing the unique work of individual botanical artists. I really appreciate the time spent by both Sally Mortimore and Nadja Guggi in honing the visual feel of these pages to best reflect my particular work and personality.

I would also like to thank my long-standing Tuesday class members, whose searching questions and enthusiasm for depicting plants have helped me explore and refine my ideas and theories about good botanical art.

And finally I would like to thank my parents, Barbara and David Bonnett, from whom I inherited my creative gifting and who encouraged me to pursue my artistic interests. This book is dedicated to their memory.

Arum maculatum

Contents

Beginnings

One Monday in September 1998 I sat down in an adult education class in South London and drew two horse chestnut conkers. This was the beginning of my journey into botanical art, a subject for which I have a passion and by which I am fascinated. On that day I knew straightaway that I had 'come home', this is what I wanted to do. I became captivated and, within the constraints of looking after young children, practised whenever I could. I soon became frustrated with having to clear the kitchen table at mealtimes, so I found a corner in a bedroom in which to tuck a desk.

That significant autumn date was not, however, the first time that I had drawn. I had always loved drawing as a child. In fact, I went to art college in order to pursue a life in illustration. But it was not fashionable at the time to depict subjects in such a literal, analytical way, so I put aside my ambition to be an illustrator and tried to get to grips with graphic design instead.

It's ironic that I stopped drawing for well over a decade as a direct result of going to art college, but once I discovered botanical art I was on track again and have not looked back or, for that matter, to the left or the right. I enjoy exploring contemporary ways of depicting botanical specimens, and constantly seek to expand my knowledge of the subject and of the potential of watercolour as a medium. Alongside this I teach, and relish the challenges this brings. It helps me evaluate the 'why' and 'how' of my own work and how I can best encourage students to find their personal style and expression within the subject.

I haven't yet arrived – and don't expect to – but long may the 'happy ever after' continue!

Botanical art and this book

The class I attended in those early days was called 'Botanical Illustration'. All I knew about the subject was that it involved plants – hence the 'botanical' part of the course title – and that we were probably going to draw them, given the 'illustration' part. Beyond this, I was totally unaware of the subject and its historical importance. For instance, the earliest herbals contained accurate illustrations to aid identification and selection of the correct plants for specific medicinal uses. Later, botanical illustrators would have accompanied explorers such as Captain Cook and worked alongside botanists to record in detail the amazing range of newly-discovered plants. Specimens collected on such trips would have been dried and pressed, so the painted illustrations provided crucial information about the colours of the plant and its typical growth pattern.

The recent revival of interest in botanical art shows no sign of abating, especially now that students of this art form all over the world can study under renowned botanical artists, thanks to online courses and tutorials.

Scientific accuracy is still a defining feature of modern botanical art. The form, colour and detail of the subject must be delineated meticulously, though this need not be at the expense of an artistic approach. In fact, I consider botanical art to sit somewhere between art and science, with some exponents pushing the genre more towards the artistic end of the spectrum and other artists leaning more towards science.

The decision as to what to include in a painting will depend on its final destination. If an artist is working with a botanist, or an illustration is needed for identification purposes, then the complete lifecycle of the plant – from bud to berry – may need to be illustrated on the same page, perhaps including dissections. If a painting is destined for a contemporary botanical art exhibition, it may be acceptable to capture a moment in time or show just part of a plant, as long as what is shown is accurate and detailed. In either case, whether focusing on a more aesthetic or

scientific presentation, the subject is usually considered on its own merits and therefore shown against a plain, most often white, background.

While I occasionally produce what might be described as a scientific illustration, I am more often than not enticed by less than perfect subjects, such as autumnal leaves, fading flowers or seed heads. In these cases, the challenge is to capture the nuances of colour or fragility of a petal in a way that celebrates something that might otherwise be assigned to the compost heap. I have experimented with depicting my chosen subjects larger than life and have placed flowers and fruit against black backgrounds in order to create glowing contrasts. The results of these explorations have been grouped here according to the different projects or exhibitions that I have taken part in.

One of my favourite shows to exhibit watercolours has been the Royal Horticultural Society's (RHS) Botanical Art Show in London. The name and nature of this event has changed and been tweaked almost every time I have been involved, but the overall purpose of the show remains the same: top botanical artists from around the world display a set of drawings or paintings on a theme of their own choosing which are then judged and awarded medals, the level of which depends on the quality both of the botanical and aesthetic aspects of the artwork.

Over the years I have seen the standard of work at this show – and the demand for space – rise and rise; the increase in demand may be the reason why the minimum number of paintings required has decreased from eight to six. I've exhibited eight times with the RHS since 2001 and love the continuity and focus of working on several paintings under the same theme, not to mention the development and exploration of ideas as the projects progress. The RHS Lindley Library now owns five of my paintings. Having gained four gold and four silver-gilt medals, I am now endeavouring to wean myself off the show by having a trade stand at the back of the hall instead.

There is another major UK botanical art show to take part in: it is run by the Society of Botanical Artists (SBA), who select a staggering number of paintings for display at its annual exhibition. In recent years I have also sent work to the US for an international exhibition curated by the American Society of Botanical Artists (ASBA).

You will see a selection of entries for all these shows over the following pages, and further images grouped together under some of my favourite themes, such as fading flowers and leaf portraits.

Occasionally I work on one-off, private commissions and bigger projects, such as the British Flora illustrations for Royal Mail Post & Go stamps issued in 2014. A range of images in these categories have been included here which, with one or two exceptions, have all been executed in watercolour.

As a teacher of botanical art my subjects sometimes reflect what we are studying in the classroom. I love teaching, not least because of the energising contact with other people which provides balance and contrast to working alone in a studio. I also value it because it helps me analyse my own processes in tandem with tutoring students.

Over the years I have developed various ideas and theories about what makes a good botanical painting or illustration, and how to bring a range of subjects to life. The Technique Diary at the end of each section in this book gives an insight into some of this thinking and the processes involved.

Finally, while this book does not set out to be a 'how-to' manual, it is intended to provide both insight and inspiration to students of botanical art and plant lovers alike.

Section 1
Larger than life

Larger than life

Fading flowers observed

My adventures in painting desiccated flowers came about because of other commitments. The beautiful cut flowers sitting on my desk were fading in front of my eyes because I didn't have the time to paint them straight away. Often, when I finally did have time, they were already past their best; and so I started painting them at this stage.

The advantage of depicting flowers that have dried out is that they don't really change any further, allowing plenty of time to work on a painting. I also became entranced with trying to depict the fragility and elegance of the fading flowers.

I decided to study six flowers at this stage of their life and exhibit my findings at the RHS London Botanical Art Show in 2012 under the title 'Larger than Life'. I scaled up the plants to give the paintings greater impact and allow the detail to be more easily observed. Each painting was 75×50 cm. Although I had misgivings on the night before the show opened, the paintings were well received, sold promptly and were awarded an RHS Gold medal. The two paintings seen here now reside in the RHS Lindley Library.

Fading Anemones
The specimen used for the uppermost flower of this pair was actually a white flower, but I also had a blue desiccated flower and felt that one blue and one red flower would more accurately reflect the common anemone hues. I used the shape and form of the white flower but painted it in the colours that I saw in the blue flower.

Desiccated Clematis
Before it could complete its natural life cycle, this clematis flower dried on the plant – rather than wilted, as one would expect – due to an unseasonally hot day.

Fading Anemones

Opposite page:
Desiccated Clematis

Fading Iris

The ovary of an iris, where the seeds develop, is normally obscured by leaves, but here it can be seen below the flower as an oblong capsule made up of three fused chambers. An ovary in this position is described as 'inferior'.

Fading Daffodils; Fading Tulip

Opposite page:
Fading Iris

Fading Daffodils

Daffodils in bud are upright but turn at a 90-degree angle to their stems as the flower opens. Once they have been pollinated, the flower returns to the vertical position seen here.

Other fading flowers

Since painting the Larger than Life set of fading flowers in 2012 I have painted many other dried flowers. I have several boxes of such specimens waiting to be depicted; sometimes I get given flowers by friends and students with the declaration, 'I was about to throw these out but thought of you!'

All these images were painted at a scaled-up size because the original specimens tend to shrink quite a lot through the desiccation process.

Opposite page:
Desiccated Texas Flame Tulip

Enduring Elegance – Desiccated Tulip;
Enduring Elegance – Desiccated Rose

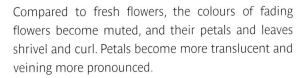

Compared to fresh flowers, the colours of fading flowers become muted, and their petals and leaves shrivel and curl. Petals become more translucent and veining more pronounced.

Translucent petals

When a petal is translucent, areas that would normally be in shadow, for example under the curl of a petal, may actually be lighter than expected. I sometimes add a backlight to my subject to enhance this effect.

Veining

Little inconsistencies in the lines will enhance the appearance of crumpling desiccation. This can be achieved by not making neighbouring veins too neat or parallel.

Drying flowers

The process of drying flowers is somewhat haphazard, in my experience. I have tried leaving flowers in their vase with and without water to fade naturally, and I have put them in the airing cupboard to speed up the process. Some flowers seem to co-operate better than others; those that have dried well can be seen in this book. I tend to dry far more than I need so that I can use the ones that are most pleasing in shape.

Loose parts

Desiccated flowers are fragile: parts such as the stamens or petals may fall off during the painting process. Including these loose parts in the painting creates movement in the composition and further emphasises the flower's delicacy.

Section 2
Nature in waiting

Nature in waiting

Rosa rugosa Hips

Opposite page:
Conkers

This set of six paintings depicts subjects that all have the potential for new life. Given the right conditions, a new generation of plants will be produced from the seed heads, together with the bulb and buds, which burst back into life once winter is over.

Each subject was enlarged by three or four times its original size to engage the viewer and to draw attention to the details of these otherwise ordinary subjects. After all, while most of us can see the beauty in a flower, we may not expect to see a daffodil bulb or winter twig celebrated for its aesthetic qualities.

Seed heads are designed to disperse their seed so I was initially frustrated, while studying some of these subjects, by the seeds dislodging. Eventually I decided to embrace this feature and include the wayward seeds in my composition; I think the images look livelier as a consequence. I do enjoy the way pictures can evolve like this.

These watercolours were awarded a gold medal at the RHS London Botanical Art Show in 2013.

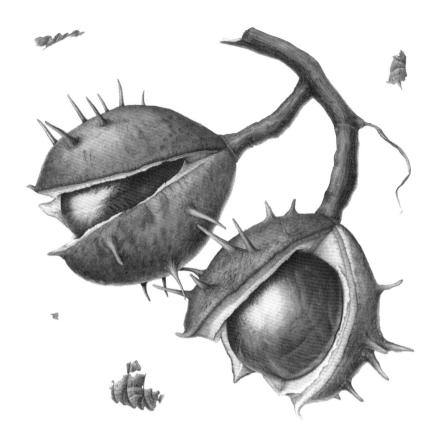

Rosa rugosa **Hips**

I chose this specimen because birds had started to eat one of the hips, and I liked the exposed fleshy interior and seeds. Including falling seeds and stamens completed this square composition and gives movement to the image.

Conkers

While painting conkers at this enlarged size I really enjoyed exploring the markings and depth of their rich chestnut colours.

Daffodil Bulb

Opposite page:
Magnolia Branch

Hippeastrum Seed Head

Opposite page:
Tree Peony Seed Heads

Tree Peony Seed Heads

This was one of the first paintings in the set where dislodged seeds were incorporated into the composition. Having decided on a square format for the series, I placed these extra bits and pieces in obvious spaces to fill out the pages.

Hippeastrum **Seed Head**

I had grown flowers from this bulb – commonly known as an amaryllis – several times, but this was the first time I saw a flower head that had gone to seed. The seed head was given to me by a student when it was still green. By the time I came to paint it, the green pod had turned brown and split open, revealing the papery seeds. The seeds are designed to be dispersed by the wind so it didn't take much for them to come loose. As I only wanted to depict a couple of the loose seeds I eventually resorted to clear glue to prevent any more from escaping.

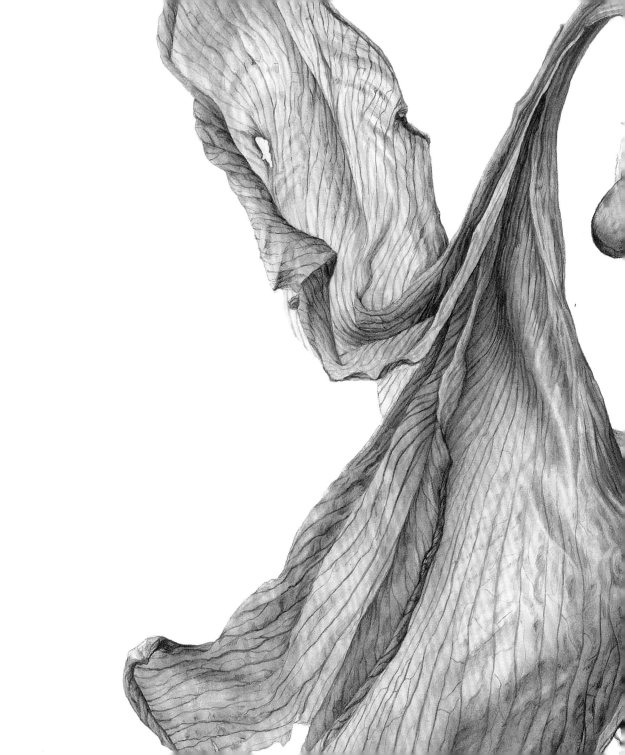

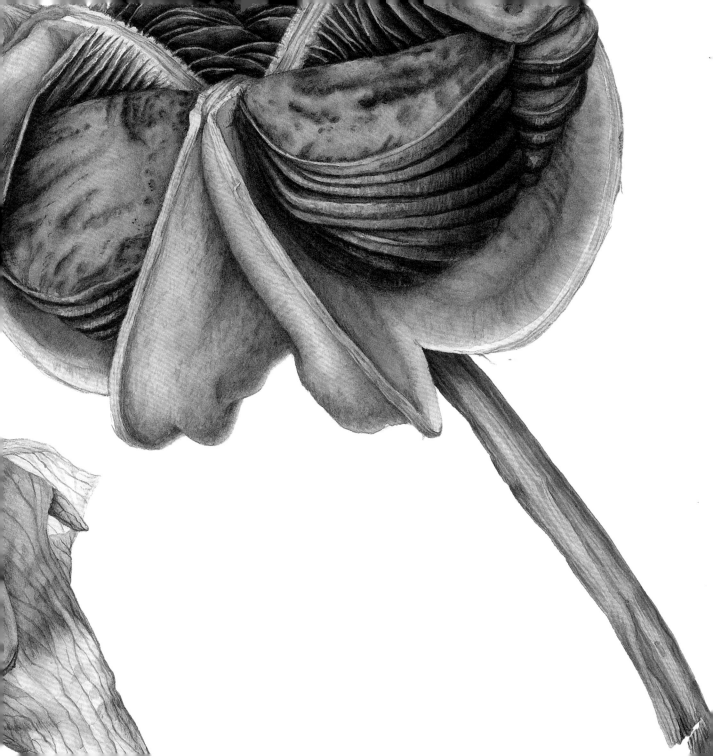

Dried seed heads and flower heads

Magnolia Seed Head;
Magnolia rostrata Seed Head

Opposite page:
Cynara cardunculus
(Dried Cardoon)

The pattern and detail of these brown specimens fascinate me. Though overwhelming at first glance, there is a rhythm to how the different parts fit together – arranged in a shallow spiral in one direction and a steeper spiral in the other. Lightly marking the path of these spirals can be a good way to start plotting out such a complicated subject.

Magnolia rostrata Seed Head

When drawing the complicated pattern of shapes on this unusual seed head, I found it helpful to mark one of central shapes on the specimen with a dressmaker's pin. This acted as a guide when I started to lose my way. A piece of re-usable adhesive could do the same job.

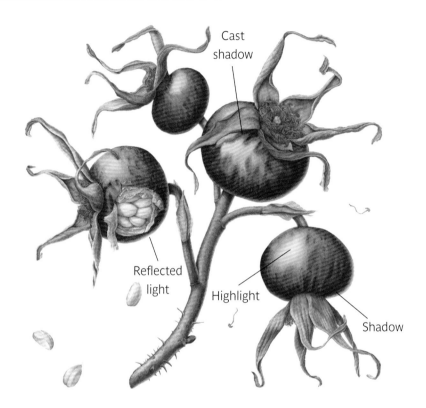

Cast shadow

Reflected light

Highlight

Shadow

Highlights and shadows

How a specimen is lit can be key to making it look more three-dimensional. Working in a studio means the artist can control this with the use of artificial lights or by working near a window. Capturing the play of light, together with a good tonal range – from highlights to darkest shadow – will create convincing shape and form on the fruit and bring it to life.

I try to be consistent in how I light all my subjects, usually from top left. In this way I have become familiar with where I would expect to see high-lights – on the top left – and shadows – mainly on the right side of the fruit. If the painted fruit doesn't look convincing enough, I can strengthen these areas accordingly.

Depicting brightness

I will often start a painting of bright red fruit or flowers with an initial layer of yellow, which glows through subsequent layers. It is worth being bold with the yellow as a pale wash won't have any affect.

For the shadow and darker areas I gradually use cooler reds, then touches of purple, rather than reaching for other favourite shadow colours. I feel that by sticking with red-biased colours the fruit stays looking bright.

Reflected light

The areas of the fruit further away from the light source get progressively darker; but there is likely to be other, diffuse light on the subject which results in a small strip of reflected light along the edge of this otherwise dark side. I try to include this reflected light as it can make the fruit more convincingly three-dimensional. Sometimes I even include it if I can't see it on the specimen.

Cast shadows

When two objects overlap, one may cast a shadow on the other. Accurately depicting the cast shadow helps to clarify the position of the two objects relative to each other. In an earlier version of the largest rose hip, seen here, I placed a cast shadow directly under the left brown sepal. This made it look like the sepal was sitting directly on the fruit. By moving the cast shadow away from the sepal, I was able to create a sense of space between the sepal and the rosehip.

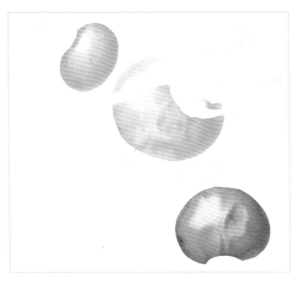

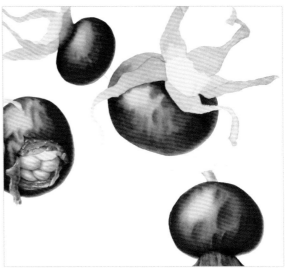

Section 3
Leaf portraits

Leaf portraits

Overleaf:
Leaves from Bath Botanical
Gardens

Laurel Leaf (*Prunus laurocerasus*);
Autumn Oak Leaf (*Quercus robur*)

Opposite page:
Shape, Pattern, Structure
– Ivy Leaf

During my years working as a tutor, I have often heard students say that they don't enjoy, or have trouble, painting leaves. In response to such statements I decided, some years ago, to investigate leaves further to see if I could get to grips with what makes them come to life and how to create an attractive leaf portrait. You can see the fruit (or foliage!) of this endeavour over the next few pages.

With the exception of 'Shape, Pattern, Structure – Ivy Leaf', all the leaves you see here were painted life-size. Unfortunately, earlier pictures were painted and sold before I was in the habit of scanning my work, so although I have included a selection of studies here I don't have a comprehensive record of all my leafy works of art.

I have been awarded two RHS gold medals for sets of leaf portraits, and three of my leaf paintings were purchased by the RHS Lindley Library.

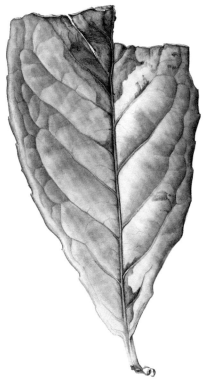

Autumn Horse Chestnut Leaf
(*Aesculus hippocastanum*);
Dried *Magnolia grandiflora* Leaf

Opposite page:
Dried Fig Leaf – Underside
(*Ficus carica*)

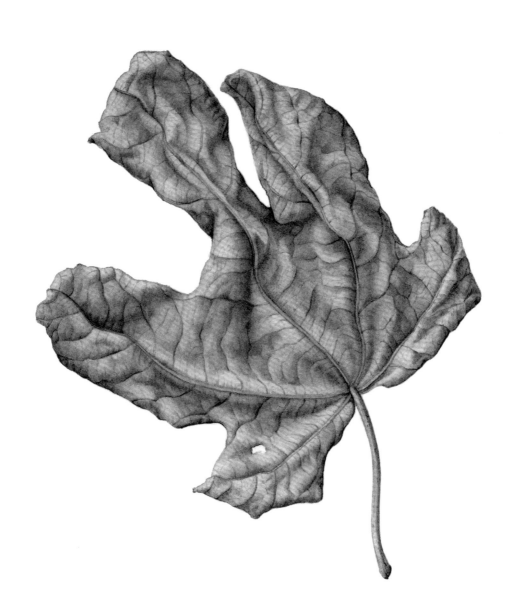

Decaying Ivy Leaves (*Hedera helix*)

Opposite page:
Bramble Leaf (*Rubus fruticosus*)

Dried Holly Leaf (*Ilex aquifolium*);
Dried *Fatsia japonica* Leaf (detail)

Opposite page:
Hollyhock Leaf (*Alcea rosea*)

Dried *Fatsia japonica* Leaf (detail)

This is one of the first leaf portraits that I completed. It is significant as it led to the decision to submit a set of leaf paintings for the RHS show in 2006.

Hollyhock Leaf (*Alcea rosea*)

This watercolour, along with the Autumn Oak Leaf and Bramble Leaf paintings, now resides in the RHS Lindley Library archives.

Shiny leaves

If a leaf has a slight 'v' profile, I often find that the side of the leaf facing away from the light source is mostly dark, while the other side is mostly light. This may mean painting quite dark areas right next to light areas. You need to hold your nerve when doing this!

To ensure a leaf looks truly shiny, I leave more light than feels comfortable at first. I can always fill in these highlights later if they appear too stark. They may need a wash of the palest blue or green, depending on the leaf.

If the leaf still isn't looking shiny enough I may need to make the dark areas of the image yet darker to increase the contrast these dark tones provide. This makes the highlight areas seem even lighter and the leaf appear shinier.

Any thickness of the leaf can be shown by painting a relatively pale edge on the darker side of the leaf and a darker edge on the mostly light side.

Textured leaves

For a cushioned leaf such as this decaying foxglove leaf or the primrose leaf below, I work on one whole side of the leaf at a time. I look for the overall form or colours in this section of the leaf and paint these using the wet-in-wet watercolour technique, that is, wet colour dabbed onto wet paper (*a.*).

Once I am happy with the overall shape or autumnal colours, I will begin to work on the individual sections between the lateral veins. I darken one side of each section to make them look cushioned (*b.*)

Finally I will use drier techniques to define and shape each small section and create the right amount of cushioning. It is important to continually refer back to the original leaf as these shapes are mapped out because they can easily become inaccurate or stylised (*c.*).

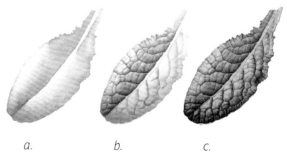

a.   *b.*   *c.*

Section 4
On black

On black

Parrot tulips

Tulipa 'Rococo'

The inspiration for these tulip watercolours with black backgrounds came from research for teaching, discussions with other artists working in this way, and a visit to the National Gallery in London where 17th-century Dutch paintings show flowers set against dark surroundings. Tulips were highly prized at this time and were often included in the bouquets depicted in these paintings.

Contrary to appearance, these images are not painted on black paper. Instead, the background colour is added to the already executed watercolour painting, as explained later in more detail. In this way, the transparent, glowing quality of watercolour on white paper can still be exploited.

Having invested so much time in the careful depiction of the flowers and their accompanying parts there was, of course, the risk of spoiling the paintings when adding the background but as I cut my teeth depicting fruit and leaves in this way, I knew how striking the result could be. Having committed myself to the black backgrounds, I was really pleased with how the framed pictures looked when I exhibited them at the RHS Botanical Art Show in 2014.

Tulipa 'Rai';
Tulipa 'Estella Rynveld'

Opposite page:
Tulipa 'Orange Favourite'

Tulipa 'Blumex';
Tulipa 'Black Parrot'

Opposite page:
Autumnal Oak Leaf on Black II;
Exotic Fruit – Figs on Black;
Exotic Fruit – Pomegranates on Black

Flowers, leaves and fruit on black

A selection of other subjects, painted with a black background.

Ben Brown Auricula on Black;
Common Poppy on Black

Opposite page:
Nasturtiums on Black;
Pear on Black;
Physalis on Black

The pictures in this section were painted in water-colour on white paper in the usual way. The black background was added at a later stage: this process suits me better than painting on coloured paper, where my favoured watercolour techniques would not work.

The black background is painted using gouache (body colour), an opaque paint that dries to a matt finish and contrasts with the luminosity created by transparent watercolours on white paper. The effect is a little like that of a stained-glass window. It is this contrast that creates the optical illusion of a richly glowing flower or fruit. It is worth noting that subjects with warm colours – reds and oranges – give better results than, say, blue and purple flowers: in combination with black, these can appear quite cold and uninviting.

I have experimented with various ways of producing these paintings, for example by painting the black area first and leaving a blank shape for the watercolour image. I found that I was picking up black gouache from the edges of the blank area and contaminating the watercolour, so now I prefer to paint the subject in watercolour first and then add the black background at a later stage.

The gouache is diluted to the consistency of single cream and painted carefully around the edge of the image. A reasonably large brush can then be used to cover the rest of the background quickly. Although patchy when wet, gouache is quite forgiving and, in

my experience, dries nice and matt. Even so it is not unusual to require a second coat, best applied at the very end of the project since the black surface is easily marked if not handled carefully.

After the application of the gouache background the image often needs strengthening as it inevitably looks quite different on black compared with the original surrounding white.

Simple shapes such as a pear, fig or a few grapes are good subjects to start out with as they are not so fiddly to paint around.

On the advice of my picture framer I tend to use dark frames for these pictures as they allow the subjects to take centre stage and really 'glow' in contrast to their dark surroundings.

Section 5
Royal Mail
Post & Go stamps

Royal Mail Post & Go stamps

In 2013 I was commissioned to paint illustrations of British flora for Royal Mail Post & Go stamps to be issued in three sets the following year – Spring Blooms, Symbolic Flowers and Winter Greenery.

The poppy image from the Symbolic Flowers set was re-issued in autumn 2017 to commemorate Remembrance Day, and the Winter Greenery stamps were re-issued for Christmas 2017.

Each original watercolour was A4 in size before reduction.

This was a fascinating project with a series of firsts for me: I worked on images that were to be reproduced at a very small size, which meant exaggerating detail and creating clear compositions; I painted the coloured backgrounds separately and then added them digitally; and, largely having been used to working alone, now I worked with and for a team of people, which I really enjoyed. The process and pitfalls of producing these stamps for the Royal Mail is documented in more detail in *Plant Portraits by Post* (Two Rivers Press, 2014).

1st Class
up to 100g

Lesser Celandine

– BRITISH FLORA I –
SPRING BLOOMS

1st Class
up to 100g

1st Class
up to 100g

1st Class
up to 100g

1st Class
up to 100g

1st Class
up to 100g

1st Class
up to 100g

– BRITISH FLORA II –
SYMBOLIC FLOWERS

1st Class
up to 100g

1st Class
up to 100g

1st Class
up to 100g

1st Class
up to 100g

1st Class
up to 100g

1st Class
up to 100g

— BRITISH FLORA III —
WINTER GREENERY

2nd Class
up to 100g

Common Ivy

2nd Large
up to 100g

1st Class
up to 100g

1st Large
up to 100g

All sixteen Post & Go stamps
from the British Flora series,
issued in three sets:
Spring Blooms, Symbolic Flowers
and Winter Greenery

The way a subject is arranged on the paper is important as this will be the first thing that attracts a viewer to a picture. I consider what or whom the painting is for. A scientific illustration that needs to show the whole life cycle of a plant may have certain size or layout constraints compared with a picture destined for a contemporary art exhibition (or stamps!).

Before deciding on a final composition, I draw out the plant components on separate pieces of cheap paper or tracing paper. This allows me to experiment with different arrangements. Several quick thumbnail sketches would do the same job.

Classic composition guidelines

I consider the following to be guidelines rather than rigid rules, but they are worth bearing in mind in order to avoid accidental composition errors.

- Positioning the main focus of a picture off-centre is better than putting it too close to an edge, or right in the middle of the page.
- An odd number of elements is generally preferable to an even number.
- Elements just touching each other, or the edge of the frame, create an uncomfortable focus. It is better either to separate the elements out, or overlap them more obviously.
- Gaps or holes in the centre of a painting should be avoided. Reposition elements or change the direction of stems to fill spaces if appropriate.

- Even if the subject has straight stems, they will look more natural if they are given even the slightest of curves.
- Crossing stems can create an unwanted focus. If you can't avoid them, keep the angle of the cross shallow.

Modern compositions

Modern compositions may intentionally disregard the classic guidelines to create fresh, or cutting-edge layouts. I have sometimes employed one or more of the following ideas to create a picture with a more contemporary feel.

- Movement can be created by angling a subject.
- Including 'bits', such as dislodged stamens or seeds, adds further movement and shows the fragility of a specimen.

- I pay attention to the spaces between the depicted items (the negative spaces), especially if there are lots of elements, or if I am filling a page. Curving stems to fit or echo the shapes of their neighbours may result in a more pleasing layout.
- Repeated elements give pattern or rhythm to the composition.
- Depicting some elements in graphite gives more depth to a picture. The graphite elements will recede. (This technique can also be used in scientific illustrations to depict the less important parts of the plant).
- I like to experiment with the shape of the paper. Influenced by social media formats such as Instagram, I currently favour square compositions.
- Cropping images can create intrigue. I use two L-shaped pieces of card and lay them on my initial drawing or thumbnail, moving them in or out to visualise different crops.
- Playing with scale is fun. Drawings can be enlarged on a photocopier or scanner.
- Depicting a subject from an unusual angle or with dramatic lighting may produce unconventional but interesting results.

Section 6
Commissions
and other paintings

Commissions and other paintings

It is great to be commissioned to portray a particular plant or flower. Although I might not have chosen to depict the subject myself, I sometimes develop an affection for these specimens during the process of study and painting.

Cedar of Lebanon, Bath Botanical Gardens

The local botanical art group was putting together an exhibition about trees and I had promised to contribute a picture, but the date of the exhibition drew ever closer without me putting pencil or brush to paper. I knew that I wanted to work on a full-size piece of paper (approx. 85 × 60 cm) and that my subject would be a skeletal tree; I had also decided I wanted to work in black and white. I was considering using pen and ink but, as time was short, I decided to attempt using charcoal as it can quickly cover a large area, unlike pen.

First I set about creating the form of the tree trunk and sprayed this with fixative before working on the texture and detail of the bark. Although I hadn't used charcoal for many years, I was pleased with the result, and the drawing sold. Following the exhibition, I was delighted to be commissioned to draw another tree in a similar style, and this second charcoal tree drawing was nicknamed (and then titled) 'Syd' to reflect the subject, a Sycamore tree.

Syd

Overleaf:
The Last Rose

Opposite page:
Cedar of Lebanon,
Bath Botanical Gardens

Benton Caramel Iris

This iris was painted for a project depicting bearded irises bred by the artist Sir Cedric Morris between 1933 and 1960. Several botanical artists were invited or requested to take part in this project and a list of possible irises distributed. We visited the gardens where the Cedric Morris irises were growing so that we were able to work from life as well as collect a flower stem and corm to bring home for further work. I chose the Benton Caramel iris for the challenge of capturing the dark, velvety petals. It took several practice attempts to get these looking right.

Claire's Peony

I might not have chosen such a complicated, multi-petaled flower if I had not been asked to paint this peony by a friend. The many petals and the richness of colour, particularly in the crevices, proved particularly demanding. I had to use the watercolour quite dry – mixing the pigment with just a little water and applying it in tiny strokes with the tip of a brush – so that I could layer up the areas of intensity without disturbing earlier applications of paint.

Heather's Sweet Peas

This painting was commissioned as a fiftieth birthday gift. As you will have seen, I tend to focus on one or two choice specimens, so the planning stage for the composition of this painting was far more complicated than usual. Once I had familiarized myself with the typical structure and flowers of a sweet pea plant, I drew several flowering stems on separate pieces of thin paper. These were then laid on watercolour paper and moved around until I was happy with their placement, at which point I traced the final arrangement onto the watercolour paper. This initial stage took many hours of planning as my aim was to distribute the various flower colours across the painting without compromising the botany and natural growth habit of the plant.

Heather's Sweet Peas

Opposite page:
Benton Caramel Iris;
Claire's Peony

Fungi – *Stropharia aurantiaca*

Opposite page:
Common Poppy *(Papaver rhoeas)*
– A Botanical Study

Common Poppy (*Papaver rhoeas*) – A Botanical Study

In May 2018, 25 countries simultaneously exhibited paintings of their native flora in a historic botanical art event, Botanical Art Worldwide. This common poppy painting was my contribution to the British exhibition. I decided to create an image that reflects traditional botanical art by including every stage of the plant's life cycle and arranging these elements in the style of a classic botanical illustration. I drew out each part separately on thin paper, cut out the drawings and then tried several different arrangements until I was happy with the composition. I was aiming to fill the space without making the placement of features appear awkward or contrived. Several of the elements were painted twice their actual size to give the painting more impact, and annotated in pencil to clarify these enlargements. This painting was used on some of the exhibition publicity.

Fungi – *Stropharia aurantiaca*

This is one of several fungi that I painted some years back. My eyes were first opened to fungi one autumn after joining a botany field trip class. I had never really noticed them before, but the range of these fruiting

bodies just astonished and captivated me, and with the tutor's blessing I began collecting specimens to paint. The fungi for this painting were gathered one damp afternoon from the flowerbeds on a golf course, where they were growing in the wood chippings.

Crimson Glory Vine

As a member of the Chelsea Physic Garden Florilegium Society I aim to paint a specimen from the garden every year to contribute to the Florilegium's archives. I am a big fan of painting leaves, so I tend to leave the more flowery plants to other members of the group and focus on subjects such as this vine. I drew out the elements on tracing or thin paper and moved these around until I was happy with the composition. Although I have shown all the stages of the plant's life cycle, I think it is obvious that the aspect I enjoyed most was depicting the autumnal colour of the large leaf.

Fern Crozier *Polystichum* sp.

One spring I noticed this tiny green fern crozier emerging from the brown foliage of the previous year's growth. Ferns are so unlike other members of the plant kingdom, and I wanted to capture this sense of 'otherness'. To enhance this notion, and to show as much detail as possible, I painted the fern crozier in isolation and magnified it to five times the size of original specimen.

The unique challenge was how to depict the downy scales in which the fern crozier is covered. I spent some time working out how I could represent these scales, experimenting with different techniques. I could have painted them with white gouache at the end of the painting process, but I felt that this would compromise the integrity of the transparent watercolour. I therefore decided to use masking fluid, applied onto the initial drawing. Once dry, I was able to proceed with painting without having to worry about the surface texture.

This painting was awarded the bronze medal at the American Society of Botanical Artists' 'Weird, Wild & Wonderful' exhibition in 2014.

Crimson Glory Vine

Opposite page:
Fern Crozier *Polystichum* sp.

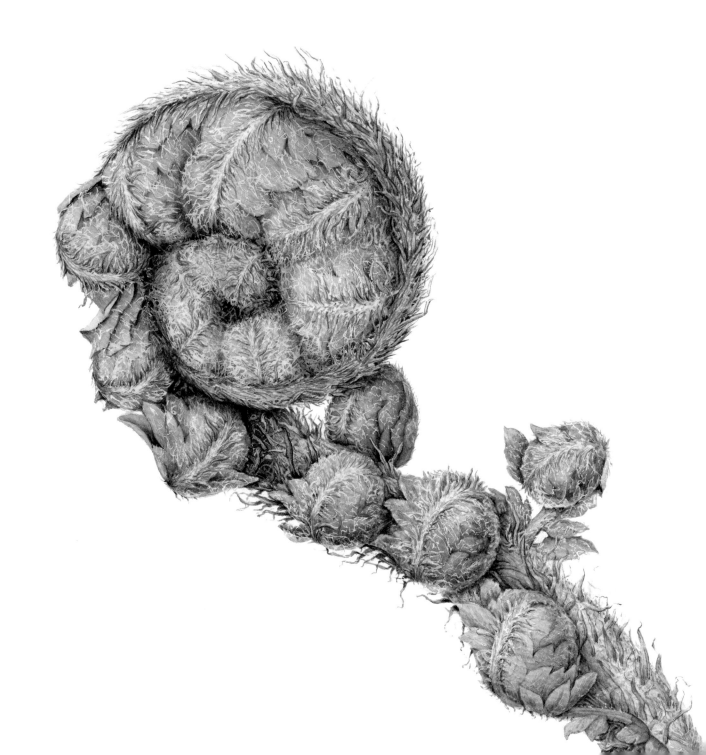

Red Polyanthus

Opposite page:
Vintage Winter Treasures (small)

Vintage Winter Treasures (small)
The background for this image is intended to suggest a vintage feel, alluding to the texture and markings of calf vellum or faded book pages. It was created by thoroughly wetting white watercolour paper and then dropping cream and pale brown watercolour onto the wet paper. The different winter elements were painted on this coloured background once the paper was completely dry.

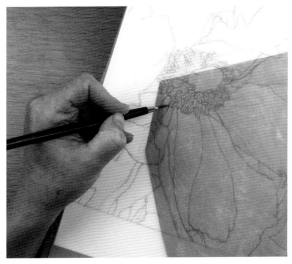

The fading anemone flower painting on the cover of this book is used here to illustrate the stages and techniques that I favour when producing botanical watercolours.

Tracing

I tend to draw the image on tracing or cheap paper initially. When I am happy with the drawing, I use transfer paper to transfer it onto watercolour paper.

Masking

At the outset I decide if any part of the image needs masking before I start painting. In this case I have applied masking fluid to the centre of the flower and the stamens so I can wash background colour over this area without having to work around these small shapes. Masking fluid is also used on the back of the petals and stem to create a hairy texture. I favour the more liquid masking fluid and use a ruling pen (shown here) or drawing nib to apply it.

Petals

To create the form of the petals I use my favourite watercolour technique: wet-in-wet. I wet each petal with clear water and, when it has just a surface sheen but no sitting water, dab in the colour and the shadows. I repeat this process on every petal, often needing to revisit each shape a second or third time to strengthen areas or add colour. The main rule is to leave each layer to dry completely before applying the

next, and to retrace the shape carefully with the new wash of water.

At this stage I also wash a range of shadowy colours over the masked area in the centre of the flower to create depth behind the stamens.

Veining and shadows

To add detail such as the veins on the petals, small amounts of stronger paint are applied with the tip of the brush. I then run damp colour down the side of these veins to help them blend into the wet-in-wet layers. Similarly, I will use small amounts of damp colour to strengthen areas such as shadows. Getting a good range of tones from light to dark is one of my priorities, whatever I am painting.

Once I'm happy with the depth of colour behind the stamens, I remove the masking fluid. The shapes revealed in this way can look quite stark and might need refining.

Stamens

To paint the stamens, I start by washing greys and beiges over the shapes then, with careful reference to the real flower, add detail to each shape. The centre of the flower is the area to which the eye is drawn so it needs to be painted with particular care.

Having worked up-close on the detail, stamens and the leafy collar, I take a step back to assess whether I need to adjust the balance of tones. Holding the picture up to a mirror is a good way to check this, or I will revisit it with a fresh eye a few days later.

Happy ever after

Opposite page:
Protea study: work-in-progress

The intent of this book was to be a visual feast, bringing you up-close to the beauty and detail of nature through my botanical watercolours. The paintings here illustrate some favourite projects to date and act as an overview of my botanical art journey so far. Though this is by no means a comprehensive catalogue of my work, it shows my progression over twenty years as I have explored different subjects and styles of presentation. Consequently, at times I have been known as 'the leaf lady', and at others as 'the painter of big, dead things'. With respect to the latter paintings, I have indicated which plants have been portrayed larger than life in the text. Otherwise, most subjects have been painted life-size even if they don't appear so on these pages. Not being systematic by nature, I don't have detailed records of titles, sizes and dates for all my works, and it is only in recent years, with advances in technology, that I have become methodical about having paintings professionally scanned.

I have been lucky enough to travel with my work, and my teaching has taken me as far afield as New York and Moscow. I was also one of a select group of worldwide botanical artists who spent some time in Transylvania recording native plants for the Transylvania Florilegium.

To keep up with my botanical art explorations beyond the date of this book, look for 'Juliatrickeyart' on Facebook, Instagram and Etsy. Other information, including class details, can be found on my website: www.juliatrickey.co.uk.

I have also produced some video tutorials – recorded as and when I have ideas, time and inclination – which can be found at: juliatrickeyart.teachable.com.

Profile

Awards

2016 Bates Award for Excellence, ASBA 19th Annual International Exhibition
2014 RHS silver-gilt medal for 'Parrot Tulips on Black'
2014 New York Botanical Garden bronze medal,
        ASBA 'Weird, Wild & Wonderful' exhibition
2013 RHS gold medal for 'Nature in Waiting'
2013 St Cuthberts Mill Award, SBA exhibition
2012 RHS gold medal for 'Larger than Life – Fading Flowers Observed'
2011 Highly Commended for Joyce Cuming Presentation Award,
        SBA exhibition
2010 St Cuthberts Mill Award, SBA exhibition
2009 RHS silver-gilt medal for 'Fading Beauty'
2008 RCHS silver medal for watercolours of leaves
2008 RHS gold medal for 'Leaves – Celebrating Imperfection'
2006 Kirstenbosch gold medal for South-African native plants
2006 RHS gold medal for 'Leaf Portraits'
2004 RHS silver-gilt medal for 'Fungi'
2001 RHS silver-gilt medal for '*Streptocarpus* species'

Memberships

Society of Botanical Artists
American Society of Botanical Artists
Bath Society of Botanical Artists
Fellow of the Chelsea Physic Garden Florilegium Society

Opposite page:
Vitis vinifera 'Purpurea',
Chelsea Physic Garden archives

Work held

Shirley Sherwood Collection, London
Hunt Institute for Botanical Documentation, Pittsburgh, PA
Royal Horticultural Society (RHS) Lindley Library, London
Chelsea Physic Garden Archives, London
Transylvania Florilegium, London
Private collections worldwide

Two Rivers Press has been publishing in and about Reading
since 1994. Founded by the artist Peter Hay (1951–2003), the press
continues to delight readers, local and further afield, with its varied list
of individually designed, thought-provoking books.